START HERE

Getting Your Financial Life on Track

R.D. Norton, Ph.D.

AMERICAN INSTITUTE *for* ECONOMIC RESEARCH

Great Barrington, MA

Start Here: Getting Your Financial Life on Track

Economic Bulletin, Vol. XLIX   No. 7   July 2009

Published by:
American Institute for Economic Research
Economic Bulletin
250 Division Street
PO Box 1000
Great Barrington, MA 01230
888-528-1216
info@aier.org
www.aier.org

Economic Bulletin (ISSN 0424–2769) (USPS 167–360) is published once a month at Great Barrington, Massachusetts, by American Institute for Economic Research, a scientific and educational organization with no stockholders, chartered under Chapter 180 of the General Laws of Massachusetts. Periodical postage paid at Great Barrington, Massachusetts. Printed in the United States of America. Subscription: $59 per year. POSTMASTER: Send address changes to *Economic Bulletin*, American Institute for Economic Research, Great Barrington, Massachusetts 01230.

Cover Art and Design: Jonathan Sylbert and Jessica Shiner
Book Design and Production: Jonathan Sylbert
Editing: Mike Scion
Proofreading: Phil Murray
Cartoons: Calder Chism

ISBN 13: 978-091361067-1
ISBN 10: 0-913610-67-4

Printed in U.S.A.

Contents

ii

Introduction...
Ten Tough
Money Tasks

"Nothing contributes so much to tranquillize the mind as a steady purpose."
—Mary Shelley

YOUR "life strategy" is something you should be working on during your twenties, if not before. This means taking control of your life. It means setting, and diligently pursuing, personal long-term goals for adulthood. To put it one way, people often wonder what they will be or do when they "grow up." Well, now you're a grown-up, and directly in charge of shaping your present and future. Your goals might be academic, artistic, material—or any mix of these and other strands. For certain, these goals are personal: They are *yours*. This book can't tell you precisely what your goals should be.

But whatever your goals are, they should include, first, having the financial means to support yourself now and, second, preparing to support yourself in your later years. The intent of this book is to tell you how to set about achieving these two goals.

"Adultolescence" and Its Challenges

A PHRASE that has entered the lexicon of the English language in this new century is "adultolescence." A hybrid of "adult" and "adolescence," the term describes a phase of life of people in their twenties or even older who still are clinging to the ways of their teenage years. Perhaps they are college graduates who have moved back into their parents' home, or are still receiving heavy financial support from their family. Perhaps they are drifting through life, trying to "find themselves" or just keeping their options open. In any case, they have not yet embraced the drive for self-sufficiency that is necessary to being a full-fledged adult.

This book is intended to help younger people who are focused on taking care of themselves—who have consciously adopted the attitude that they now are adults.

The individual chapters address money-management tactics—nuts and bolts approaches to solving potential problems and organizing your financial life. Nevertheless, some generalized advice is worthwhile here at the start. So, in the manner of self-help books since time immemorial, we offer the following nuggets of free advice:

To repeat: This book is not about how to help you find your own special goals or life strategies. If you wish to read more about that quest, you could

GET A JOB. (EASIER SAID THAN DONE IN A DOWN ECONOMY.)

BE FINANCIALLY RESPONSIBLE. REMEMBER, WHEN YOU SIGN A CONTRACT (FOR A CELL PHONE, A CREDIT CARD, OR ANY NUMBER OF OTHER PRODUCTS WITH CONFUSING AGREEMENTS), YOU HAVE TO MAKE GOOD ON IT.

DON'T GET MARRIED—OR PREGNANT—TOO YOUNG. (BUT IF YOU ALREADY DID, SOLDIER ON.)

AVOID BAD COMPANY. (THIS MAY BE THE MOST IMPORTANT POINT.)

TAKE CARE OF YOUR BODY. (DON'T SMOKE, AND KEEP MOVING. AN ACTIVE BODY IS A HEALTHY BODY.)

TAKE CARE OF YOUR MIND. (THINK POSITIVE, DESPITE IT ALL. THERE IS POWER IN POSITIVE THINKING. NEGATIVE THINKING WILL GET YOU NOWHERE DESIRABLE.)

KEEP TAKING CLASSES. (FOR COLLEGE OR VOCATIONAL CREDIT, OR OTHERWISE. YOUR MIND NEEDS THIS TO KEEP SHARP.)

NEVER FORGET WHO HELPED YOU. (YOU KNOW WHO THEY ARE.)

FIND A HOBBY. (WORK ISN'T EVERYTHING!)

VOLUNTEER TO DO GOOD WORKS. (YOU WILL FIND THE RIGHT KINDS OF FRIENDS, AND CULTIVATE A FEELING OF SELF-WORTH.)

do a lot worse than to read or view Randy Pausch's "The Last Lecture: Really Achieving Your Childhood Dreams," the famous parting thoughts of a computer-science professor in his late forties who had learned he had terminal pancreatic cancer and would be dead within a few months, despite otherwise vigorous health. Pausch's book, "The Last Lecture," was a *New York Times* best-seller. His upbeat and highly engrossing lecture can be seen in two versions on YouTube: an hour-plus lecture or an 11-minute version.

Your Finances: Strategy and Tactics

As **YOU** develop your life strategy, you must decide your long-term financial goals—and write them down. Make sure these goals are specific. Just as with New Year's resolutions, a financial plan lacking specific goals is likely to be arbitrary. Moreover, the chances of sticking to such a plan are slim to none.

But listing specific goals (such as owning a house, retiring by age 70, 60, or 50, or putting two or three or four children through college) is only a first step.

Given your goals, how can you best accomplish them? The answer is in the tactics you adopt and practice: concrete plans and procedures for getting what you want, specifically in the realm of money.

Ten Tough Money Tasks

To **simplify** what can quickly become a very complicated subject, the chapters that follow are organized around 10 specific tactical issues. Here is a list of each, with a comment or two:

1 **How to Pay Your Bills on Time.** This is not just about how to slice up your income to pay various bills and debts, but more basically, how to know what bills are due when. The trick is organizing your payments in a way that works best for you. Then the benefits will overflow: control, comfort, and a good credit rating!

2 **Temptations: Credit Cards, Debit Cards, ATMs.** Credit cards are a necessary evil of today's society. But debit cards are even trickier, and ATMs also can get you into trouble. Which ones should you rely upon—and for what?

3 **Your Credit Score—And What to Do about It.** The "FICO" score you receive influences the terms and availability of loans you can take out, when the need arises. So it pays to figure out how the various FICO scores are compiled, and what you can do to raise yours.

4 **Identity Theft.** On and off the Internet, identity theft has become a growing threat. But you can take certain precautions to minimize the risk that someone posing as you will loot your bank account and run up huge credit-card bills.

5 **Car Costs—And Insurance.** It is said that the only thing teenagers will save for is to buy a car. Do they know something the rest of us don't? Probably not.

6 **Staying Alive—Health, Disability, and Life Insurance.** You have heard of health insurance and life insurance, but disability insurance is equally important.

7 **How to Avoid Financial Fraud.** As the recent case of Bernard Madoff—a once-respected chairman of a Wall Street investment firm—reminds us, Ponzi schemes can rope in just about anyone. Madoff bilked thousands of investors out of an estimated $65 billion. Knowing the red flags of financial scams, from the large to the small, can help you avoid getting snookered by a smooth-talking con artist.

8 **Couples and Money: Outsmarting Conflict.** Disagreement over money issues is a leading cause of breakups. But one remedy to remove such friction from relationships is to establish a third checking account—not yours, not your mate's, but "the house account." If you can get that account set up and functioning properly, financial harmony is more likely to follow.

9 **Retirement Planning in One Lesson.** You are likely to have to DIY it as the Social Security program crashes and traditional pensions vanish. And the sooner you can put away tax-sheltered money, the more you will have when the time comes for you to retire. While the details of specific savings programs available to you—such as a 401(k), or an IRA—can get complicated, there are some basics you should know.

10 **Where Do You Want to Live?** With house prices continuing to fall almost everywhere during the recession, there may come a time when buying a house just to live in makes sense once again. How will you decide when the time is right—and where you want to live?

1

How to Pay
Your Bills on Time

"Our necessities
never equal
our wants."
—Benjamin Franklin

"You can't always get
what you want."
—Mick Jagger

EVERYONE comes across a scrounger every now and then. In just about every social circle there's that guy or girl who always is broke. This is the person who never pays for the drinks or food when you go out, who bums rides and "borrows" cigarettes (or bicycles or iPods or clothes), who never ponies up for gas when you go on a road trip. The freeloader. This is the person who asks you to lend him or her cash (and, naturally, never pays it back).

Not surprisingly, this probably is a person who's always late on the rent, or is being evicted, or just had the car repossessed. A person who is flaky about money is not worth having as a friend, no matter how charming or funny or ridic the person is. In fact, as you've probably seen, this deadbeat eventually gets dumped by his or her pals and has to find new ones.

And guess what? When it comes to doing business in the real world, bankers and loan officers, landlords and merchants have a low tolerance for financial flakes. In fact, if you write a bad check—one with "non-sufficient funds"—you can be prosecuted.

Being fiscally responsible is a hallmark of being an adult. Paying your bills, and paying them on time, keeps you a customer in good standing, keeps you from incurring late fees that can dig a deeper hole for you, and keeps the electricity on. It also keeps you in good company—meaning, with solid friends. People of good character ("winners," in other words) don't want to be around people who are broke, bankrupt or beggars ("losers," in other words).

Well, good intentions alone won't keep you in the black instead of the red. You must live within your means to avoid incurring a lot of debt. But you also must be *organized*.

This chapter offers practical solutions to help you pay your bills on time, know what's in your checking account, and keep the financial records you actually need (so you can trash the rest).

Simple Steps to Bill Paying

THE FIRST trick to paying your monthly bills on time is to put them all in one place, by themselves, where you can find them. The second trick is getting into a set pattern of paying.

STEP 1. WHEN A BILL ARRIVES IN THE MAIL, PUT IT IN THE DESIGNATED PLACE. SOME PEOPLE FIND THAT A SHOEBOX WORKS. OTHERS PREFER THE 31-DAY CARDBOARD TRAYS THAT LET YOU ARRANGE BILLS BY THE DATE THEY ARE DUE. WHATEVER WORKS FOR YOU IS FINE. EVEN A PLASTIC BAG WILL DO.

STEP 2. GET IN A RHYTHM. SHOULD YOU PAY BILLS TOGETHER, ONCE A MONTH? OR ARE YOU MORE COMFORTABLE PAYING A SOLITARY BILL AS SOON AS IT SHOWS UP IN THE MAIL? OR IS THERE A HAPPY MEDIUM, SUCH AS PAYING THEM ONCE A WEEK, ON SATURDAY MORNINGS, SAY? NONE OF THESE TACTICS IS RIGHT OR WRONG. THE ONLY REQUIREMENT IS THAT YOU KEEP TRACK OF WHEN PAYMENTS ARE DUE SO THAT YOU CAN AVOID LATE FEES AND OTHER INCONVENIENCES.

STEP 3. CONSIDER PAYING ON LINE—EITHER BY REGULAR PRACTICE, OR AS A BACKUP. IF YOU SOMEHOW OVERLOOK A BILL (OR HAVE BEEN AWAY TRAVELING OR SIMPLY SLAMMED BY AN OVERLOADED SCHEDULE), IT HELPS TO BE ABLE TO GO ON LINE AND MAKE A PAYMENT THAT DAY, THROUGH A TRANSFER FROM YOUR CHECKING ACCOUNT OR ON A CREDIT CARD. WITH ANY LUCK, THAT WILL ALLOW YOU TO PAY A BILL LATER THAN USUAL WHILE STILL AVOIDING LATE FEES AND A TARNISHED REPUTATION.

STEP 4. CONSIDER SETTING UP AUTOMATIC PAYMENTS. SOME PEOPLE PREFER TO "AUTOMATE" THEIR MONTHLY PAYMENTS TO THE MAX BY USING EITHER ON-LINE OR REGULARLY SCHEDULED ELECTRONIC FUNDS TRANSFERS FROM THEIR BANK ACCOUNTS.

This latter option is what the telephone or cable company has in mind when it says on the envelope your bill comes in, "Want to save a stamp?" On the bill inside is a box you can check to automate your monthly payments, along with a line where you can enter your bank information. This information will include your bank *routing number* (the one at the bottom left on your paper check) and your individual *account number* (the one in the middle).

The benefits of this four-step drill are huge. For one, it makes you a responsible, organized bill-payer who never falls behind. For another, making payments on time, you build up your credit record. (We'll discuss your credit score in Chapter 3.) In addition, paying your bills in this orderly fashion gives you a reality check on your monthly payments—and whether you are spending more than your income.

Yet another benefit from seeing where your money is going each month is to allow you to become a disciplined saver. A time-honored strategy for building up personal wealth is "paying yourself first"—regularly putting money away from your income. Once you have a solid grip on your monthly bills, you can consider making an automatic savings deposit each month.

But none of those good things can happen until you decide what works for you to get the bills paid on time. Until that happens, your finances will be slightly (or seriously) out of control.

Do You Need to Make a Monthly Budget?

Is **THIS** matter of figuring out your own preferred style of bill paying really just a beginning version of making a budget? In a way, yes. As already noted, paying your bills alerts you to how much you are spending each month—and whether you are spending more than your income.

In a perfect world, these calculations would lead you to create a monthly budget. You would start by writing down your monthly income. Then you'd write down and keep track of all your monthly spending. You would compare the two figures, and resolve to not spend as much as you earn. In other words, you'd stay within your budget and have something left over each month, either to save or to pay down whatever debts you have.

But the reality is that few people actually design step-by-step budgetary plans. So if you feel the same aversion to budgetary discipline, you are not alone.

On the other hand, if an out-and-out budget is the thing for you, here are two good educational resources that can help you start:

GO ON LINE TO HTTP://MONEY.CNN.COM/MAGAZINES/MONEY-MAG/MONEY101/LESSON2/. LESSON TWO IS ABOUT "MAKING A BUDGET."

THE AIER BOOKLET, "SENSIBLE BUDGETING WITH THE RUBBER BUDGET ACCOUNT BOOK," PROVIDES GUIDELINES AND WORKSHEETS. YOU CAN ORDER THIS $8 BOOK AT (888) 528-1216, OR AT WWW.AIER.ORG/BOOKSTORE.

How Much Is in Your Checking Account?

IT USED to be easier to balance a checkbook. All you had to do was write down every deposit made and every check you wrote. True, you also had to keep track of your ATM (automatic teller machine) withdrawals. But that just meant holding on to the ATM receipt and entering it into your checkbook as a reduction in your bank balance.

All that was before people started using debit cards to write "instant checks" for payments large and small, right down to drugstore or newsstand purchases of a dollar or two.

The problem is that three different kinds of actions may overwhelm your fragile checking account. The checks you write, the ATM withdrawals you make, and the debit-card transactions all reduce the checking account balance.

The simple—and crucial—solution is to *write down every transaction*. Keep the receipts not only for ATM withdrawals but also for all the debit-card payments you are racking up. Then set a time every day, perhaps in the evening when you're home and going through your wallet, to enter the deductions in your checkbook.

Paperwork You Must Keep— And Paperwork You Can Toss

YOUR monthly bills aren't the only paperwork you have to keep track of. Some documents you need to keep on file in a safe place because they are vital records for you. But the good news is that much of the paperwork you have to manage can be tossed almost immediately.

Now, some people are very organized, and can probably find gainful employment as clerks, if that's their desire. They are good at keeping records and putting documents in a place where they can be readily retrieved. But most people are not, either because they're not organized by nature, or they just don't feel it's worth the trouble.

Let's say you're in the latter group, not really excited about neatly filing away receipts and credit-card bills. In that case, what is the bare minimum of pieces of paper (or computer records) you need to hold on to?

See "Five to Keep or Toss" on the next page for answers.

Five to Keep or Toss

Here are five categories of paperwork—from stuff you can toss almost right away, to material you need to keep filed permanently for your own protection:

1 **Disposables.** These are items you can typically throw away without regret: routine bills that have been paid, including utility and phone bills and food receipts such as from groceries and restaurant meals.

2 **For tax purposes.** Hardcopy bank statements, in case of a tax audit, plus the previous seven years of tax returns. Meaning: If a return is more than seven years old, you can throw it away.

3 **"Semi-permanent papers."** Insurance policies in general: what you are paying and what they say they will provide, should it come to that. Loan agreements—the terms of how you are to repay a loan, and what will happen, say, if you repay the loan early. Warranties for products, so that if a gadget (or a car) goes wrong, you will have the piece of paper that says it has to be paid for by the seller.

4 **"Forever papers."** These include a birth certificate, college transcripts, diplomas, marriage certificates, a current passport, a Social Security card.

5 **For homeowners (and renters).** A home inventory of assets (preferably backed up by video) is essential, so that in case of fire, flood or other disaster, your home-insurance policy claims can be substantiated.

Speaking of fires, floods, and disasters, where should your records and documents be stored? Whatever is worth keeping is worth protecting, perhaps in a fireproof safe at home. Copies of legal or financial documents and agreements can be left with a lawyer or in a safe-deposit box in a bank, as backup.

For a fuller treatment of this question, you can read Chapter XI, on handling records, in AIER's 2009 edition of *How to Avoid Financial Tangles.* (You can order the $12 book at the toll-free number or website listed previously in this chapter.)

One last point on record-storing…

About every six months you should empty out your wallet and photocopy all the cards and documents stuffed into it. That way, if you lose your wallet (as many of us do, eventually), you will know exactly what needs replacing— or canceling.

Keeping Track of Paperwork Is Worth the Trouble

IS ALL of the above too much trouble to take care of? Not when you consider what is at stake. Keeping close, accurate tabs of your financial life is your personal power. Your financial health is the image you present to the world. You want to be a person who has his or her act together.

By paying your bills on time and keeping track of your checking account, you'll have a much better chance of handling the random expenses that keep popping up. And you'll have a much better chance of never being a scrounger, a deadbeat, a freeloader.

Just think about the people you know who always need to borrow money— or need you to pay the check in the restaurant. Don't be one of them.

Now that we've covered how to organize your bill paying, we'll look next at three types of transaction vehicles that most of us use, but which can be subtle money drains.

> "He that does not
> economize will have
> to agonize."
> —Confucius

2

> "I say that the strongest
> principle of growth lies
> in human choice."
> —George Eliot

Temptations:
Credit Cards, Debit Cards, ATMs

YOUR friends are planning a spring trip to the Bahamas, and you're dying to go, but your funds are short. It's all you can do to scrape by each month. But there is a way you could swing the airfare and lodging: by whipping out the plastic. Even though you're paying off a hefty balance on your credit card already, you still have enough left on the limit before maxing out. Some of your friends tell you they're using their cards themselves. You're sorely tempted; you tell yourself you'll whittle away at the bill after you get back, and it will all be worth it. Who wants to stay behind in your same old town when everyone else is off partying in some exotic locale?

Credit cards are a necessary evil. On the one hand, they encourage short-sighted behavior and overspending. On the other, they are all but indispensable for such basic transactions as renting a car. What's more, when using credit cards for transactions, laws are in place to protect you from credit-card errors and even fraud. If you buy something with a credit card and it turns out to be defective, you probably have a better chance of getting your money back than if you had paid in cash.

This chapter looks at decisions as to when to use a credit card. We discuss some of the safeguards for credit cards and compare them to the less secure alternative of debit cards. We also alert you to common "gotcha" tactics banks frequently use to hit ATM and debit-card users with stiff overdraft fees.

The Road to Ruin?

CREDIT cards pose two special temptations. One is the cards' easy availability to college students. The other is the low minimum monthly payment requirement.

Ironically, college students with little income often have a simpler time getting a credit card than many other individuals seeking credit for the first time. Card companies court students, regarding them as potentially high-earning, long-term customers with good repayment records—especially since parents are likely to pay the bills if their children don't.

According to a recent study by the Sallie Mae Foundation, 84 percent of college students have a credit card, compared to 67 percent in 1998. These students carried an average of $3,173 in debt, excluding student loans.

In some unfortunate (and by no means rare) cases, such lingering debts may cause the first step toward a debt cycle that can overpower recent college graduates. In this scenario, those who are financially strapped sometimes obtain cash advances on one credit card just to make payments on other card accounts.

This situation often involves a sad downward spiral for the card holder. The borrower ends up devoting a significant portion of after-tax income to paying credit-card interest and other charges—income, in other words, that cannot be spent on regular living expenses, much less put away in savings.

What this ultimately means is that, in exchange for what turns out to be a relatively brief acceleration of consumption, the debtor has a permanently lowered standard of living.

Perhaps the greatest risk of credit—and one that all too many credit-card holders in our society have showed they are willing to assume—is the mass of debt that builds quickly with slow repayment.

Making just the minimum payment each month on a credit-card balance will stick you on an endless and frustrating financial treadmill. If you were only to pay the 2 percent minimum payment on a $5,000 balance on a card with an APR (annual percentage rate) of 11 percent, it would take more than 23 years (and $3,979 in interest payments!) to pay it off. In contrast, if you were to increase the monthly payment to $250, the balance would be paid off in 23 months at an interest cost of $549.

College Debt

THEN there are the student loans—the dead elephant in the living room. This is one of the biggest obstacles to financial freedom that people in their twenties face today. Recent college graduates are said to carry an average of $20,000 in college debt (not including what may be accrued by those who go on to graduate school).

Realistically, then, college debt and credit-card debt, together, can add up to a veritable mountain of financial obligations, just as you are trying to get started in your career.

As if the typical debt burden you leave school with were not enough of an obstacle to financial freedom, a recent book exposé on college loans suggests that just as with credit cards, lenders are just waiting to pounce when you make a late payment. In *The Student Loan Scam: The Most Oppressive Debt in U.S. History—and How We Can Fight Back* (Beacon, 2009), author Alan Michael Collinge, founder of the grassroots organization StudentloanJustice. Org, charges student-loan companies with a litany of abuses that he contends cry out for reform.

All we can add here is that the double whammy of student loans and credit-card debt is likely to dominate the budgeting decisions of many recent graduates.

What follows is a framework on how to handle credit and debit cards—so that you do not take on any more debt than you have to.

Pay as You Go?

THE FINANCIAL crisis and recession of 2008-09 seem to have led many people to change their thinking—and habits—regarding credit cards. Along with frugality in general, cutting back on credit-card usage began to seem fashionable. This twofold shift has meant spending less, and using cash or debit cards more.

Not surprisingly, using your credit card less will tend to make it easier for you to cut down on your buying. "With cash, your spending ability is limited," Paula Peter, a professor of consumer behavior at San Diego State University, told *Wall Street Journal* writer Jennifer Waters in a timely article published in January 2009. (The article was headlined, "Yes, You Can Live with Less Plastic.") A related point is to make specific plans for what to buy before you shop, rather than just cruising the mall, ready to shop on impulse.

In practice, shifting away from credit-card purchases requires people to use ATMs or debit cards more often. Both options tap directly into checking accounts. An ATM withdraws cash, while a debit card draws down the balance for a specific payment. So long as you request when setting up your account that no "overdrafts" on your account be honored, the net effect will be to pay as you go. (More on this point in a moment.)

Weaning yourself off of frequent, large and/or spontaneous expenditures with your credit card means you'll reserve paying with plastic only for a few specific purchases, with a view to paying off your entire credit-card balance every month. That way, you can build a credit history (a subject of Chapter 3) while avoiding the interest costs of carrying a big fat balance from month to month.

When would paying with a credit card make sense? One example might be paying for airplane flights or other big-ticket items, especially where frequent-flyer miles or other rewards programs are in play. This allows you to build up rewards points over time, while still waiting until the end of the month to pay the card balance off in full. Another example is making an unexpected or emergency payment (such as if your car dies on you) that might otherwise wipe out the balance in your checking account. Your objective in this scenario would be to pay off the balance in as few months as possible—both to minimize interest costs and to get you back on the pay-as-you-go wagon.

Take Charge of Your Checking Account

THERE are several drawbacks to this pay-as-you go approach. One is that debit cards provide less consumer protection than credit cards in the event of a disputed payment. Another drawback is that when you use your debit card to rent a car or check into a hotel, the business may put a *hold* on your checking account for more than you end up paying, making your available checking account balance temporarily smaller. The result is to make overdrafts more likely—even where there is enough money in your account to cover all your payments!

And now for a rather ugly truth: Banks *want* you to overdraw your checking account. Banks have developed surprisingly nasty arrangements to get you to do this, so that they can hit you with penalties and fees. Banks put a different spin on this. Their pretext is that they provide you, the customer, with a cushion against insufficient-funds penalties. The reality is that banks position themselves to gain much more in fees. By one estimate, such fees added up to $17.5 billion in 2007. This is a high-stakes game.

The way the game works is that with all the checks you write, ATM withdrawals and debit-card payments you make, you may lose track of your account balance. Suppose you make an ATM withdrawal or a debit-card payment, not realizing your account is low or empty. Instead of blocking your transaction, the bank may then honor the overdraft and charge high fees ($35, say, for each incident). Moreover, some banks require repayment of the "loan" and the penalty fee within a few days; additional fees kick in for any delay.

The solution is within your reach. Make sure that when your checking account is empty, your bank will reject both ATM withdrawals and debit-card payments. Simply by requesting a zero-overdraft privilege, you can avoid a potential cascade of overdraft fees and lateness penalties. By the way, this issue comes under the heading of "courtesy overdraft policies." Don't be fooled by the jargon; "courtesy" has nothing to do with it!

Credit Card Billing Errors—And How to Fix Them

CREDIT-CARD accounts are subject to a variety of billing errors that can be costly to the consumer. You should be in the habit of reading each monthly statement carefully to catch any such errors promptly. You also should keep all the receipts for items you charge, so that you can check that they appear correctly in your bill. A general rule is: *When there are entries that you find unclear, ask.*

Under the provisions of the Fair Credit Billing Act, the consumer has 60 days from the date the bill was mailed to notify the creditor *in writing* about any errors.

The law also provides that in case of lost or stolen cards, there is a limit of $50 on the cardholder's liability for each card that is used without authorization. Thus, cardholder liability is limited to $50, even if hundreds of dollars of unauthorized purchases are made.

By contrast, debit cards carry fewer safeguards against theft or abuse. In an extreme situation, a stolen debit card could enable the thief to clean our your checking account before you know the card was gone. More on such dangers in Chapter 4.

But first, we're going to look at another aspect of credit—one that serves as your financial report card. That's the subject of Chapter 3.

> "A bank is a place that will lend you money if you can prove that you don't need it."
> —Bob Hope

3

Your Credit Score —And What to Do about It

So you're finally ready to bite the bullet and get yourself a newer car, one that doesn't leave a small puddle of oil every time you pull away from the parking spot. You research on line for a good late-model used car. You know that quality will cost money, but you figure you can handle a loan from a bank or other lender as long as the annual percentage rate (APR) isn't too high and the monthly payment is not too steep.

You've never applied for a loan other than a student loan before. Now you're about to learn what your financial report card really is. It's a four-letter word: "FICO."

FICO stands for Fair Isaac Corporation, a company that gathers and processes statistical information about your credit history. Fair Isaac is at the top of a three-layered pyramid of info-gathering agencies: lots of local credit bureaus, three national credit-reporting companies, and Fair Isaac—the ultimate authority that assigns a numerical grade to your credit-worthiness.

Imperfect though FICO and other credit scores are, they can determine whether you can get, say, a mortgage loan, or how much your car loan will cost. FICO scores range from 300 to 900, with few below 500 or above 850. One analyst says the scores can be mapped out as letter-grade equivalents. These estimates appear in Table 1.

On the Fair Isaacs website (www.myFICO.com), an example shows the effect a high score can have on the cost of a loan. For two different types of

Table 1

Estimated Letter-Grade Equivalents to FICO Scores in 2008

FICO score	Letter grade
760-850	A+
700-759	A
660-699	B
620-659	C
580-619	D
500-579	F

Source: Don Taylor, "Dr. Don issues his FICO letter Grades," www.bankrate.com.

loans, borrowers with high scores were reported to have sharply better rates and lower payments.

As Table 2 shows, for a three-year car loan the difference was $300 a month. So this is another high-stakes game—and you need to know the rules.

How Lenders Score Credit

Traditionally, creditors classified risks according to the three "C's": character, capacity, and collateral. *Character* refers to how hard a borrower will work to make sure a loan is repaid. *Capacity* refers to the borrower's ability to repay, as measured by assets and discretionary income. *Collateral* is whatever the lender can claim (by repossessing a car or foreclosing on a house) if the borrower cannot or will not pay. Needless to say, considerable guesswork went into evaluating the three C's.

How do credit raters measure these variables today? You have a credit record with three national credit bureaus: Equifax, Experian (formerly

Table 2

Rate and Payment Contrasts for High- and Low-Score Borrowers

FICO score	Annual Percentage Rate, 15 year home-equity loan	36-month auto loan (monthly payment)
760-850	4.76 %	$1,587
620-639	6.35 %	$1,867

Note: Based on prevailing interest rates, March 2, 2009.
Source: "The higher your FICO credit score, the lower your payments," www.myfico.com.

TRW), and TransUnion. From their data, Fair Isaacs calculates your FICO score. Then most lenders either rely on your FICO score directly or use an "application" or "customized model" to evaluate your credit worthiness. The application or customized model combines the FICO score with data from your loan application to derive a composite score. Either type of score falls into a numerical range, indicating the risk level of a loan. The higher the score, the lower the perceived risk. The lower the risk, the lower the interest rate—as you can see in Table 2.

One thing to remember: Creditors make it part of the credit-analysis process to verify the information you supply them in an application form. Just as with a job résumé, honesty is the best policy. Exaggerations have a way of being discovered.

Getting Scored

How is your basic FICO score calculated? Among dozens of possible variables, FICO scoring relies on five factors, giving most weight to your credit history:

1 **Credit payment history** (35 percent of the FICO score). This record is probably the single most important measure of a borrower's character. Credit bureau reports contain information on delinquent payments on credit cards and loans. They look at the past seven years, and no further.

Creditors examine how serious, recent and frequent your late payments have been within the seven-year reporting period. For example, if you missed the date when a bill was due and made a 30-day late payment, it would not be as troubling as a 90-day delinquency. However, if a credit report shows that you've made several 30-day late payments in recent months, your application for a loan would probably be viewed as a greater risk than someone with a 90-day delinquency several years ago. Finally, if a pattern of late payments (even minor ones) emerges, spread across a credit history, a lender would be concerned about your ability to repay the loan.

2 **Level of debt utilization** (30 percent). Applicants who are at or close to their credit limits will generally lose points in a credit-scoring system. Statistically, borrowers who have "maxed-out" on their credit lines pose more of a risk to lenders. (Keep that in mind if let your credit-card balance get out of control.)

3 **Length of credit history** (15 percent). The more years of credit experience you have—meaning, taking out loans, having a credit card or buying on credit—the better you will score in this category.

4 **Number of new credit applications** (10 percent). Each time you apply for credit, it gets posted to a credit report as an "inquiry." Too many inquiries (usually four or more in a six-month period) will cost you points on a credit score, since people who apply for credit often have poor repayment records. In the past, consumers who have shopped around for a car or home loan would get multiple inquiries listed on their credit reports, even though they were, in effect, seeking only one loan. Credit-scoring systems now try to correct this misinterpretation by treating all applications for a car or home loan made within a seven-day period as a single inquiry.

5 **A good mix of credit experience** (10 percent). Having several major credit cards, as well as installment credit such as a car or student loan, will improve your credit score. Your ability to secure credit from a variety of reputable lenders indicates your credit worthiness. (On the other hand, a loan from a finance company—as opposed to a bank or major credit-card company—may count against you, since such lenders tend to work with riskier clients.) One note of caution, though: Because of the wave of personal bankruptcy filings and loan defaults in recent years, many creditors actually may give fewer points for possession of five or more credit cards.

To sum up: The old-school "three-C" method of rating your credit relied more on a personal judgment call, while today's credit-scoring systems analyze a lot more data, going back seven years, to determine the likelihood that you, the borrower, will repay a loan.

How to Raise Your FICO Score

HERE'S some good news if you're worried about ending up with low FICO score. If you handle your finances carefully, you can boost your score.

Under "payment history," for example, www.myFICO.com advises you to pay bills on time and make good on missed payments as soon as possible. In regard to "amounts owed," you should keep credit-card balances low and pay off debt rather than shifting it from one account to another. As for "length of credit history," people with only brief credit histories are advised not to open too many accounts right away. Tips regarding "new credit" include a reminder that you are free to monitor your own credit report. When it comes to types of credit use, you are advised to have several credit cards and several installment loans (for example, car loans), and to keep current with your payments on all of them.

Credit Reports: How to Correct Errors

LOCAL credit bureaus across the nation assemble and disseminate millions of consumer credit reports annually. Most of them store and distribute credit reports through one of the three national systems mentioned earlier. These are Equifax, Experian and TransUnion.

Fortunately, borrowers have access to the same information as the lenders. This means that you can review your credit reports to see if any errors have been made that could unfairly lower your FICO score. The Fair and Accurate Credit Transactions Act of 2003 says that you can order a copy of your credit report from each of the three national credit bureaus for free, every 12 months.

You can obtain your free reports online at www.annualcreditreport.com, which was created for this purpose by the three national credit bureaus in 2004. *This is the only online source for your credit record recommended by the Federal Trade Commission.* While other advertised sites may look and sound similar, their offers of your "free" credit report usually involve the purchase of some other product for a price. You don't have to buy anything when ordering from annualcreditreport.com. As to your FICO score, it can be obtained free at www.myfico.com (although you may be asked to sign up for a service you can then cancel).

You can order all three free reports at once, which may help you clean up any errors in preparation for taking out a new loan. Or you could space the three reports out over the course of the year, just to keep tabs on whether there are any suspicious listings creeping on to your records—a red flag for identity theft. (More on this in the next chapter.)

What if an error has been made in billing that may jeopardize your credit score? The Fair Credit Reporting Act provides borrowers some protection against erroneous and outdated credit information that could jeopardize your chance to borrow money. It gives the consumer the right to contest the items in a report that are inaccurate or outdated. The credit bureaus are required to look into your request in a timely manner and report any corrections, to clean up your record.

Your Credit Record—And Your Identity

IN SHORT, your credit record is a snapshot of your credit accounts and how you handle them. The credit-rating system is meant to measure your financial security—grading your ability to repay your loans. Whatever its imperfections, the FICO system may benefit you in an indirect way. It may just motivate you to work consciously toward earning a higher credit score. And that's the direction you should be heading, anyway: gaining control over your credit.

There is another good reason for you to keep track of your credit reports. As the next chapter explains, identity theft has soared in recent years. Your credit reports are an early-warning system when someone is trying to hijack your financial ID.

Identity Theft

"There is a powerful tension in our relationship to technology. We are excited by egalitarianism and anonymity, but we constantly fight for our identity."
—David Owens

So **YOU** get a call at home one day from a rather unpleasant person who says he's a collections officer. He has your full name and address, and even your Social Security number. He gruffly demands payment on an account for a credit card he says is six months overdue. But you've never opened an account for such a credit card. This is the first you've heard of it!

It slowly dawns on you that you are a victim of identity theft. ID theft is one of the fastest growing crimes in the United States, victimizing an estimated 8 million Americans in 2008. It occurs when your personal information is stolen and used to commit fraud—such as using your personal information to obtain a credit card, cell-phone account, or worse.

Avoiding Identity Theft

A decade ago, Congress addressed this issue with the passage of the Identity Theft and Assumption Deterrence Act. This made identity theft a separate federal crime and provided punishment of a fine or imprisonment for up to 15 years, or both. Many states also have enacted laws to criminalize identity theft. That's how pervasive and serious ID theft is. But there are ways to protect yourself. Here are 8 of them:

1 **Guard your Social Security number.** Social Security numbers are the key to your credit report, bank accounts, and other sensitive information. Employers and financial institutions may need your Social Security number for wage and tax reporting, while others, such as landlords or utility companies, may ask for it to conduct a credit check. Beyond that, giving out your Social Security number is often unnecessary. Ask why someone needs it, and what it will be used for, before you make a decision to divulge this sensitive piece of information. Never carry a Social Security card around with you.

2 **Watch for "phishing."** This is a scam done via email. Phishers send out messages that appear to be from legitimate companies (such as banks or IT administrators or social websites) saying that they are working to enhance security and prevent fraud, or need to update your account information. To help them, they ask that you re-confirm your identity by entering personal information such as your Social Security number, credit-card number or account password. They may direct you to click on a link, which brings up an authentic-looking website. As a rule, you should never provide sensitive information over the Internet unless you were the one to initiate the contact.

3 **Give personal information only to websites with a secure server.** Secure servers encrypt information as it is being transmitted so that outside interceptors cannot read it. A site with a secure server will show a locked padlock at the bottom of the browser page, while a non-secure site will show an unlocked padlock. Remember, URLs that begin with "http" are not secure. Only those that begin with "https" are secure sites to which to send sensitive information.

4 **Never give out personal information over the phone.** That is, unless you have initiated the contact. To be sure you are dealing with a legitimate source, call the company's customer-service number or check its website for any scam alerts. If you do not wish to be solicited by telephone, contact the National Do Not Call Registry at 1-888-382-1222.

5 **Use an original password, and change it periodically.** Avoid using easily available information, such as digits from your Social Security number, your birth date, or your phone number, when creating a password for your email, website or cell-phone account. Instead, think of an original yet memorable password that only you could know. Mix different character types—letters and numbers, uppercase and lowercase. Use different passwords for different services so that if someone finds out a password for one of the services you use, the ID thief cannot use it to open the door to your entire private life. Try changing your passwords at least once a year.

6 **Check your credit history once a year.** Obtaining free credit reports was discussed in Chapter 3. Many people do not find out about ID theft until they are denied loans because of actions taken by ID thieves.

7 **Pay attention to billing cycles and check your account statements.** A missing credit-card bill could mean an ID thief has taken over your account and changed the billing address to throw you off.

8 **Tear up pre-screened credit-card offers.** This is so that no one else can fill them out in your name. Better yet, call 1-888-5-OPTOUT (1-888-567-8688), a number maintained by the three credit bureaus for consumers who do not wish to receive such offers. It is also a good idea to tear up or shred your charge receipts, checks and bank statements, expired charge cards, and any other documents with personal information before you put them in the trash.

How to Recognize It

STILL, no matter how well you protect the information available about you in the mail or over the telephone or the Internet, you are still at risk for ID theft. The reason is that hackers and other criminals sometimes manage to steal credit-card and other databases that may include your confidential information. That happened to the writer of this book only a few months ago, as he learned when his bank told him they were sending a new credit card, just to be on the safe side. A similar case came to light with the arrest of a software employee who stole the credit histories of 30,000 people and sold them to a ring of ID thieves.

Unfortunately, it could take days, months or years before some of these victims become aware that their identities have been stolen. But there are certain obvious signs that you will want to recognize should it happen to you.

One indicator would be that something you expect to receive in the mail fails to arrive. This could be a bill, an account statement from a bank, tax forms or newly ordered checks.

Or you might have the opposite happen: You receive an unexpected bill for something you never purchased. Sad to say, this also happened to the writer within the past year! He was accused of having purchased a couple of items from a plus-sized ladies' retailer in the Midwest, 1,000 miles away.

Because this "mistake" showed up as a charge on a credit card he never uses, he noticed it. Since credit-card companies are legally obligated to look into disputed purchases, they have people employed solely for that purpose. So within a few months, the bogus bills for several hundred dollars' worth of dresses were erased. (On the other hand, the results of the credit-card investigation were never made known to the humble victim; he should have pursued the matter.)

Similar red flags would include unauthorized transactions on your bank statement, rejected loan applications, hostile approaches by the Internal Revenue Service or bill collectors, or unfamiliar accounts listed in your credit reports. Even worse, victims of ID theft could get arrested for crimes committed by the ID thief. All such annoyances can be straightened out, given sufficient time and money. The downside is that in the meantime you may feel like the beleaguered movie character with a case of mistaken identity.

What to Do if It Happens

F YOU become an ID theft victim, the Federal Citizen Information Center recommends that you file a report with your local police. Keep a copy of the police report, which will make it easier to prove your case to creditors and retailers. Contact the toll-free fraud number of any of the three national credit bureaus to place a fraud alert on your credit report. You only need to contact one of the three companies listed below to place an alert:

> **EQUIFAX:** 1-800-525-6285; WWW.EQUIFAX.COM; P.O. BOX 740241, ATLANTA, GA 30374-0241
>
> **EXPERIAN:** 1-888-EXPERIAN (397-3742); WWW.EXPERIAN.COM; P.O. BOX 9532, ALLEN, TX 75013
>
> **TRANSUNION:** 1-800-680-7289; WWW.TRANSUNION.COM; FRAUD VICTIM ASSISTANCE DIVISION, P.O. BOX 6790, FULLERTON, CA 92834-6790

To simplify the lengthy credit-repair process, the Federal Trade Commission offers an ID Theft Affidavit you can use to report the crime to most of the parties involved. Request a copy of the form by calling toll-free at 1-877-ID-THEFT (438-4338) or visiting www.ftc.gov/bcp/edu/microsites/idtheft. All three credit bureaus and many major creditors have agreed to accept the affidavit.

When dealing with ID theft, you can also get advice from the Identify Theft Resource Center at idtheftcenter.org. This is a nationwide nonprofit educational and assistance program for consumers and ID victims, co-founded by a woman who was a victim of identify theft.

Backup

D THEFT has become commonplace enough that insurance policies are being offered from such reputable businesses as Costco and American Express. Such insurance policies, to protect your assets if you are victimized by ID theft, resemble travel insurance—which is designed to get you out of trouble if something serious goes wrong on your journey. For an extra layer of protection, you should consider researching and possibly buying ID theft insurance from a reputable vendor. As usual before buying any insurance plan, you will want to weigh its benefits (the protection it provides) against its costs (the premiums you will have to pay).

There is one valuable possession that you are required by law to have insurance on: your motor vehicle. And insurance is just one of the big-ticket costs associated with your set of wheels. We'll look at what a car truly costs in the next chapter.

> "If you think nobody
> cares if you're alive,
> try missing a couple
> of car payments."
> —Earl Wilson

5

Car Costs—
And Insurance

So **YOU'RE** ready to buy yourself a decent set of wheels that will get you off the bus or subway or bicycle, or maybe out of the smoky, dented beater you half wish someone would steal. You're going to invest your hard-earned money only in something reliable that will carry you through the next few years as you fight your way up the economic ladder in the real world.

You've figured out how much you can spend out of pocket, and how much you can afford per month on a loan to cover the remainder of the price to get a good solid car. Well, the calculations on the ultimate cost of that car are quite different from just coming up with the figure you need to buy it. That is, if you think long term.

The Long-Term Costs of Owning a Car

Next to keeping a roof over your head, the cost of owning and operating a car—including what you must pay for insurance and gas, maintenance and registration—is the largest monthly and annual expense for many people. Table 1 on the next page shows the estimated average costs of owning and operating a motor vehicle during the course of a driving lifetime. If you average the cost of the five different car sizes in the table, you come up with a figure that exceeds $320,000. Does that surprise you? And consider this: The sum represents the costs of owning and driving just one vehicle. Two- and

Table 1

Estimating the Average Costs of Owning and Operating an Automobile in the United States for 50 Years
(current dollars)

Cost Category	Small Sedan	Medium Sedan	Large Sedan	4WD Sport Utility Vehicle	Mini-Van
			Automobile Type		
Depreciation	$78,087	$96,348	$133,784	$127,815	$101,815
Gas/Oil	70,425	92,550	99,600	127,875	105,075
Insurance	47,450	45,350	48,650	44,400	44,150
Maintenance	33,975	41,400	43,800	48,000	40,725
Taxes	20,500	28,100	34,500	35,750	28,150
Total:	**$250,437**	**$303,748**	**$360,334**	**$383,840**	**$319,915**

Note: Based on 750,000 miles of travel over 50 years; 12-year, 100 percent depreciation on autos.
Source: "Your Driving Costs," American Automobile Association, 2008.

three-car households have proportionally greater costs.

One big way to keep the cost of having a car under control—so you can have more money left over for other purposes—is by choosing the right vehicle for you at the start. As the table shows, the long-term costs of a large SUV are much higher than for a typical sedan. The SUV will eat up $383,840, while the sedan will consume $250,437. That's a difference of $133,403. But that is only the beginning of the story. The money you hadn't spent on a more expensive car could be invested during that time period, bringing you a profit on the return.

You just need to compare the entire costs—including what you would miss out on if you invested the difference—when choosing between a more expensive or less expensive car. Keep a few points in mind. Seemingly minor short-term differences in outlays for auto transportation, say $40 or $50 per month, can become very great differences over the course of 30 or 40 years. The long-term savings achieved through informed selections of the most economical cars suited to an individual's or family's needs far outweigh the one-time savings of $300 or $400 achieved through dickering in the dealer's showroom.

So when you choose a particular costly option, just remember the longer term sacrifices—either your own or your children's—that may be required. Consider, for example, that the estimated cost of four years of tuition, room, and board at a private four-year college now runs about $130,000.

Whatever your decision, there is one more point that is appropriate to make here, and it's supported by a number of independent studies: *Driving a car as long as possible* is probably the most economical practice over the long run.

Finding the Right Car, Getting the Best Deal

THEN again, there is the short run. How can you get the best deal on a car— and what cars offer the most value, balancing price and quality?

Knowing the rules of the car-dealer game can save you hundreds of dollars. Buyers need to know the actual dealer cost of a car (vs. the "sticker price"), what profit margin is acceptable to the dealer, the most economical ways to purchase options, what sales tricks to expect, how to avoid dealer add-ons and packages (such as undercoating), and how to determine a reasonable trade-in amount for your old car.

These bargaining matters are well-covered by the consumer economists at *Consumer Reports* magazine. If you are in the market for a car, consult the April "Annual Auto Issue" of the magazine, back issues of which are available in most public libraries.

About Car Insurance

EVERY state requires at least a minimum level of liability insurance, in case you injure another person or damage someone else's car or property. As Table 2 shows, however, that is only the beginning of the story.

Table 2

Average Expenditure for Auto Insurance, 2006

Nationwide average expenditure	$817
Average premium for full coverage (liability, comprehensive, and collision)	$937
Liability coverage	$489
Collision coverage	$308
Comprehensive coverage	$140

National average outlays for privately-owned passenger vehicles in 2006.
Source: Insurance Information Institute.

How Much Do I Need?

According to the Insurance Information Institute, the average car-owner spent $817 on auto insurance in 2006 (the latest year with statistics available). Those who purchased "full" coverage (that is, a combination of liability, collision, and comprehensive insurance) paid $937, on average, in premiums. Let's consider how much coverage in each of these three main types—liability, collision, and comprehensive—you should carry.

1 Liability insurance. First, and as noted, liability insurance is legally required for drivers in every state. It protects the owner of an automobile from claims for injury to people and damage to property as a result of an automobile accident. When you register a motor vehicle, the state generally requires proof of such insurance. Even the careful driver needs this coverage. The degree of coverage afforded varies in policies issued by different companies, and the minimum amount of coverage required to register a vehicle varies from state to state.

The amount of liability coverage required to register a vehicle is often grossly inadequate when you consider the vast sum you may be legally liable for in the event of a serious accident. The mandatory minimums may be as little as $15,000 coverage for death or injury to one person, with a $30,000 aggregate limit of damage for death or injury to all persons to whom the owner becomes liable in a single accident. (Such amounts are described in the jargon of the insurance industry as "15/30 limits.") The cost of this insurance varies with the locality; the kind and model of car insured; the age, gender, and qualification of the operator; and the principal use of the vehicle.

The additional premium charged for increasing the amount of coverage is proportionally small compared with the increased protection gained. For example, increasing the coverage to 100/300 ($100,000 per person and $300,000 per accident) might only double the premium from its statutory minimum.

The insurance policy you buy states the limit of the insurance company's liability. You are responsible for any legal liability in excess of that amount. The risk of loss is substantial, and automobile accidents happen even to careful drivers. It is advisable to carry at least

100/300 "bodily injury coverage." An alternative way to get higher bodily injury coverage for automobile accidents is with an "umbrella policy" for personal liability, which offers liability coverage for home and car together at generally reasonable rates (say, $200 for $1 million in coverage).

2 **Collision insurance.** Collision coverage is included in most policies to insure against damage to or loss of the automobile itself. Such collision coverage usually is subject to a deductible, which is the portion of any claim that the owner must pay himself before the insurance company pays anything. Coverage for damage incurred in a collision is costly, often accounting for well over half of a motorist's auto insurance premium.

Collision coverage can raise insurance costs sharply for new or luxury cars. It can come as a shock to a younger buyer who has paid a premium for a fancy set of wheels to find that higher insurance costs also enter the picture, effectively raising the monthly car payments.

One way to reduce the cost of collision insurance is to increase the amount of the deductible to $500 or even $1,000, from the more usual $200 or $300, so that only a relatively major accident will result in a claim for collision damage. However, that would mean that the cost of most mishaps would be paid by the owner out of pocket.

This brings up a related issue. Many companies raise the premium or even drop the insured person as an account if the person has certain number of claims of any sort. So you should think twice before filing claims for small mishaps.

3 **Comprehensive insurance.** A comprehensive auto policy gives protection primarily against loss of a vehicle from fire and theft. But it also includes protection for loss due to practically any other hazard (except collision), including windstorms, tornadoes, hailstorms, floods, and acts of vandalism. The additional cost of such comprehensive coverage over the premium for plain fire and theft coverage is nominal. Insurance companies grade geographical locations according to the number and severity of the accidents occurring in each. These factors determine the premium rate for any single location.

"No-Fault"

INCIDENTALLY, a number of states have "no-fault" automobile-insurance stat-utes. There are substantial differences in these laws among the states, but the common feature is that victims of an automobile accident who suffer bodily injury must recover their financial loss from their own insurance company rather than from another party. No-fault statutes in some states also apply to property damage losses. The no-fault feature applies to losses of specified amounts or less. Recovery for losses above these amounts must be made under the usual provisions of insurance and law. Ask your insurance agent if there are such laws in your state, and how they work.

Renting and Car Insurance

WHAT about when you rent a car? You may not need the insurance that car-rental agencies offer, which tends to be expensive. So before renting a vehicle, check with your own insurance agent (whose card belongs in your wallet, with a phone number, in case of an accident) to find out whether you need to purchase the insurance the car-rental agent is obligated by law to offer you. Either way, make sure you are covered. The same dangers (liability and collision) you face when driving your own car are also present with a car rental.

By the way, a third option for insurance on a rental car is the offer some credit-card companies make. If you pay for the car rental with a given card, you may receive free insurance from the card company as part of the transaction.

In sum, you should have the broadest possible insurance coverage and be sure that anyone else authorized to drive the vehicle is properly licensed and qualified to drive under the terms of the policy. Know the terms of coverage and what may void them, and see that everyone authorized to drive the car also is fully instructed on these matters. Anyone who drives, or even rides in, a vehicle that is not properly insured is running an unacceptable, and usually needless, risk.

The Bottom Line

THE long-term *financial* aspects of car ownership are just as important as the dickering over the sale price, and the mechanical upkeep, of owning a car. You will need to decide "how much car" is consistent with a solid financial plan. If your auto-related expenditures dominate your monthly budget, then you may be mismanaging your financial affairs—no matter how good the bargain you struck on the purchase price.

For more on these issues, including detailed ratings and comparisons of different makes, you might refer to AIER's annually updated publication, *What Your Car Really Costs.*

6

> "Death is nature's expert advice to get plenty of life."
> —Goethe

Staying Alive with Insurance Coverage

UNLIKE liability insurance for your car, health-related insurance is seldom if ever required by law. But you definitely need medical and disability insurance. So this chapter is intended to help you figure out what coverage works best for you, given the costs.

For most young people out in the workforce, health-related insurance coverage depends largely on employer benefits. This is notoriously the case for health insurance, and it tends to be true for disability insurance as well. Life insurance is also a benefit some employers provide. In some cases, you will want to supplement such coverage. For the unemployed, of course, the task gets more formidable: how to maintain (and pay for!) continuous coverage between jobs.

In any case, even when younger workers have jobs, they may be tempted to go without health-related insurance. The cartoon in this chapter reminds us that accidents can happen. So can unexpected but costly illnesses—which can afflict even "young and healthy" people.

Consider the 28-year-old New York City woman who worked as a receptionist and didn't want to pay for insurance. That was fine until she experienced stomach pain that would not go away. It turned out she had diverticulitis (which, like other kinds of tummy aches, can be difficult to diagnose—opening the door to various expensive tests). The bill for her 46-hour stint came to $17, 398. As she put it, "I could have gone to a major university for a year.

Instead, I went to the hospital for two days." (Alanna Boyd, quoted in Cara Buckley, "For Uninsured Young Adults, Do-It-Yourself Health Care," the *New York Times*, February 18, 2009.)

The good news is that you may not need life insurance yet.

Life Insurance?

TO BE real, the question here is this: Is someone near and dear to you dependent on your financial support, and would that person suffer hardship if, against all odds, you died. If so, you might want to consider taking out a life-insurance policy naming this person as a beneficiary.

On a similarly somber note, if no such dependent needs your financial protection, the only life insurance you might require would be for "final expenses," which is a nice way of saying burial costs.

If your goal is to protect loved ones against the loss of your income, you are probably best served by a straight *term insurance* policy. As the name implies, the premium (cost) purchases coverage only for a specified period ("term"), such as 20 years. Crucially, term insurance is renewable for additional term periods (possibly at higher premiums) *without a medical examination*. Otherwise, you could lose the ability to get life-insurance coverage if your health fails (which is increasingly likely the older you get), just when you would most need it. The premium for each renewal period depends on the policyholder's age at the time of renewal.

In other policies, variously known as *whole, permanent, or universal* life insurance, the premium is larger than a similar amount of term insurance would be for someone of the same age, but the premium's rate remains the same as long as the policy remains in force. The initial excess premiums (the cash value of the payments you pay for the policy above the cost of insurance) are invested by the insurer.

The bottom line: You don't need it. There are better ways to invest your money.

What you will need, once you have financial dependents, is a term life-insurance policy that pays from four to 10 times your annual income. If your employer does not fully provide that coverage, you will need to go out into the marketplace and shop around. Your advantage will be your youth. A 30-year old non-smoker, for example, should be able to get 10-year term insurance paying a death-benefit of $100,000 for about $200 a year.

Disability Insurance

DESPITE the sound of it, this is not medical insurance. Instead, disability insurance benefits are designed *to replace earnings* in the event that the insured person is physically unable to work. In most instances, a worker who is severely disabled by accident or disease will be covered by Social Security, with monthly payments determined by the worker's prior earnings and the number of dependents. ("Severely disabled," in this instance, indicates impairment so extensive that you cannot perform *any* substantial gainful work for at least 12 months.) Other types of income supplements may be available, but most are inadequate. For example, workers' compensation policies, which most employers must carry by state law, will pay only in the event of an accident or injury sustained on the job, and the benefits tend to be low.

A good disability policy is a worthwhile investment. The most common flaw in personal-insurance programs is *a lack of balance between disability insurance and life insurance*. Many people who have adequate life-insurance protection carry little or no disability insurance. Without adequate disability insurance, a loss of income because of protracted sickness or injury may be financially devastating.

Unfortunately, unless offered by your employer, disability insurance can be expensive. You should have coverage equal to 60 percent of your income. If you earn $50,000, this would suggest $30,000 in coverage, which might run as high as $1,000 per year if purchased individually.

Health Insurance

NOW WE come to the hard part. As noted earlier, health insurance for most working-age people gets down to what their employer offers. That may mean they either fall through the cracks (have insufficient or no health insurance) or consciously choose to "self-insure," meaning they find an insurer themselves and pay out of pocket, or do without. A survey from the Kaiser Family Foundation found that 13 million young (19-29) adults had no health insurance in 2007. This was 29 percent of the 45 million uninsured Americans that year. More recently, the issue has heated up during the Subprime Recession because younger workers who lose their jobs may be especially likely to forego coverage.

Now let's consider six scenarios for workers and non-workers:

Six Health Insurance Scenarios

1 You have a job. The cost of your health-insurance policy will vary depending on the type of plan, how much your employer contributes toward coverage, and the state you work in. According to another survey by the Kaiser Family Foundation, in 2008 monthly health-insurance at mid-sized to large companies averaged nearly $400 a month for individual coverage and over $1,000 a month for families. The employee-paid share of these policies averaged $64 a month for individual coverage and $248 a month for families. In some states, of course, the figures ranged higher.

2 You've just lost your job, and your former employer provided health insurance. You can continue coverage under COBRA (an acronym for a law Congress passed in 1985: The Consolidated Omnibus Budget Reconciliation Act). If you enroll in COBRA within two months of leaving your job, you can continue your coverage for 18 months. The problem with COBRA has been its expense, since unemployed workers had to pay for the entire premium, including the portion that the employer had paid before. This can easily exceed $500 a month just for individual coverage.

(In early 2009, as part of the American Recovery and Reinvestment Act, Congress voted to pay for 65 percent of a newly unemployed worker's COBRA expenses. This subsidy was available to workers who lost their jobs between September 1, 2008, and December 31, 2009. To qualify for this program, an individual's annual income could not exceed $125,000, or $250,000 for a married couple. The 65 percent subsidy was made available for nine months, to meet the needs of the continuing economic crisis of 2009.)

3 You lack employer coverage, perhaps because you are self-employed. It generally is difficult and expensive for a person to purchase basic health insurance on his or her own, directly from an insurer. But it can be done. The problem is that such individual plans are costlier than group plans as a rule, because group plans benefit from the pooling of risk.

4 You are not working and have child dependents under age 19. You may be able to take advantage of a nationwide program called the Children's Health Insurance Program. CHIPS is designed for those who are not eligible for federal Medicaid and who have limited or no health coverage. For a small monthly premium, the program provides benefits such as hospital care, physician services, prescription drugs, and drug-treatment services. States have different eligibility rules, but in most states, uninsured children 18 years old and younger whose families have incomes below a specified threshold are eligible. For more information, visit the U.S. Department of Health and Human Services website: insurekidsnow.gov.

5 You're interested in remaining covered by your parents' health insurance. Some states have extended the age for which 20-somethings can be covered by their parents' health insurance. Health insurance under this category used to be open only to students, and only up to age 21. More recently, eligibility has been extended to non-students, and the age when parents can still list their children as dependents for this purpose has risen to 26 in some states. To learn more, contact your parents' insurance carrier.

6 You trust in fate. Like the receptionist afflicted by diverticulitis, millions of Americans lack any health insurance. They are known in the insurance industry, perhaps unfairly, as the "young invincibles"—a term that implies a conscious decision not to spend precious money on health insurance that they believe they will not need.

For some members of this optimistic group, going uninsured will amount to a de facto "catastrophic coverage" policy, one in which the emergency room is the solution to a catastrophe. By law, staffs in emergency rooms must treat the seriously sick or injured, regardless of the patients' ability to pay. But this isn't exactly a foolproof plan for the uninsured, because massive debt can follow.

Where to Find Help

BEYOND employer-provided policies, insurance is sold to individuals by "agents," meaning salespeople acting as agents for specific insurers. Or it is sold by "brokers," who sometimes are referred to as "independent agents," meaning that they do not work as an agent for any one company but rather can sell policies form a variety of insurers, acting as a go-between for the insurer and the insured. Agents and brokers earn a living by taking a commission on the policies they sell. Not that this necessarily influences their advice to you. But it might. They are better off selling you more insurance—perhaps more than you need.

Many people now use the Internet to comparison shop for insurance, especially for life insurance. These sites have some drawbacks. Visitors typically must fill out an extensive information form to get quotes. The results page may display only a handful of quotes from certain companies that participate on a particular site, not from a very broad universe of potential insurers. Worse, some sites are little more than marketing tools used by insurance companies and agents in order to generate sales leads. If you give your address or phone number to such sites, you are likely to be contacted by several agents.

Two things you want to make sure of: 1. The insurance company will still be around if you have to make a claim. 2. It will pay a valid claim reasonably quickly. As to the first, the A.M. Best Company rates the financial strength of insurance companies. A Best's Financial Strength Rating (FSR) is the firm's opinion of an insurer's ability to meet its obligations to policyholders and provides a useful tool for consumers to compare the financial stability of various companies. Ratings—which range from A++ and A+ (superior) to F (in liquidation)—are available at ambest.com/ratings (registration required). As to the second, check the Consumer Information Source of the National Association of Insurance Commissioners (at naic.org) to research company reputations for paying claims.

Once you agree to purchase an insurance policy, you pay the premium to the insurer and the insurer sends you a written copy of the policy. Review it thoroughly to see if the coverage you got is what you wanted. The policy also should tell you how to file a claim. In addition, watch for conditions that invalidate or cancel the coverage. Examples of activities that can invalidate your life insurance include skydiving, obtaining an airplane pilot's license, or racing dirt bikes.

What if the written policy is not what you expected? As we noted earlier, for these and other insurance-related disputes, including claims, a good first step is to go to the website provided by the National Association of Insurance Commissioners: www.naic.org. You can find information for a particular state at www.naic.org/state_web_map.htm.

Salud

THEN again, if you are lucky you may never have to rely on your insurance policy in a crisis. Insurance is perhaps best thought of as something you have to have but hope never to use. As the Spanish toast puts it: *!Salud, amor, dinero—y el tiempo para disfrutarlos¡* ("Health, love, money—and the time to enjoy them.") The better your insurance protection, the better your chances of enjoying life.

7

How to Avoid Financial Fraud

"Honest people don't hide their deeds."
—Emily Bronte

"The key to acting is sincerity, and if you can fake that you've got it made."
—Jeff Bridges

THE DOORBELL rings. Outside your door stand two smiling young people who appear to be in their late teens. They ask how you're doing today, ask your name, shake your hand, tell you their first names, and then say they're students trying to raise money for a trip to Europe. They're selling magazine subscriptions. They've already sold some to your neighbors. And, by the way, what's your next-door neighbor's name?

You figure out pretty quickly, from their speech, that they're not from your town, or even your state. In fact, they don't look that well dressed or well washed, either. Sort of like they've been traveling on the cheap. Moreover, they don't sound very educated. You rather doubt they can even name three nations in Europe.

Your better instincts tell you that this is a hustle. Still . . . you feel a jolt of compassion as they show you a list of magazines and say they'll take cash or a check, and they promise you'll be getting the magazines within a week.

These kids seem friendly and harmless—and what if their cause actually is legit? Turning them down flat would make you feel rude and uncool. Do you lie and tell them you're too broke? Or do you actually cough up some cash, giving them the benefit of the doubt?

You wrestle with this dilemma, briefly, then impulsively fish in your wallet for a $20 and hand it over for a subscription to *Rolling Stone*. You jot down your name and mailing address on a form, and tell them to keep the change.

They thank you warmly, which makes you feel good.

By the next day, though, the pang of pity you felt for that pair has been replaced by an irritating sense you've been conned. This only increases after you relate the story to a friend, whose first and only comment is, "Are you serious?"

Victims and Perpetrators: In All Shapes and Sizes

WE DISCUSSED identity theft in Chapter 4. Well, ID thieves are only one species of the scam artists out there in our cruel, insincere world.

Fraud is an act of deceit or trickery by one party—the perpetrator—intended to induce another party—the victim—to part with something of value. What sorts of characters orchestrate fraud? Who are their victims?

The key factor in victimization, according to the National Institute of Justice, is simply whether one is exposed to an attempt. Thus, getting defrauded can happen to anyone.

Surprisingly, younger people are more likely to be victimized than older people. Seniors apparently are not the trusting and compliant victims that law-enforcement authorities and the media portray them to be. Similarly, better-educated people are more susceptible to fraud than you might think. The NIJ study found that the people least likely to succumb to fraud were those without a high school diploma, and those with graduate degrees. The group most likely to fall prey had some college or an undergraduate degree.

There is no simple explanation for these findings other than the conclusion that a formal education does not necessarily make one "streetwise."

Fraudsters vary as much as the victims they target. They come from every educational, geographical, racial, religious and socioeconomic background, from each gender and a broad range of ages. They may be a stranger or a friend. Some may be quite visible in the community, while others remain hidden in the shadows. They may operate out of a plush office, a "boiler room" with a bank of telephones, or a suitcase. So beware—con artists come in all shapes, sizes, and colors. Don't rely on a single stereotype to send up a red flag.

But there are a few characteristics that many—though not all—swindlers share. One is a well-documented past. Checking into it may save you both money and grief. Another is the swindler's reputation as a smooth talker, which is notorious and well deserved. The swindler's ability to avoid saying anything personally disagreeable or offensive comes from being a good lis-

tener. But when the initial chitchat is over and the conversation turns to the opportunity at hand, the swindler's act is well rehearsed.

The scam can be for a small bit of money—such as the price of a supposed magazine subscription—or for many millions of dollars in a high-end investment scheme. Consider, for example, the recent Madoff case, apparently the largest Ponzi scheme in American history.

Ponzi Schemes, Madoff, and Healthy Skepticism

ONE OF the puzzles regarding the estimated $65 billion scam that Bernard Madoff is said to have run is how so many otherwise informed and intelligent investors could have been duped for so long. In a Ponzi scheme, early investors are paid high returns with money collected from new investors—not from earnings on actual investments. These early investors believe their money has been invested wisely and that they are enjoying real profits from the financial markets. They have no clue that the money they are receiving in the form of profits is simply the investment capital from subsequent investors.

Madoff was a well-connected founder and chairman of a nearly half-century-old Wall Street investment firm, and a respected philanthropist with strong standing in the financial community. His firm boasted a long list of prestigious clients, including banks and investment funds, colleges and charitable foundations, lawyers and real-estate developers, a major newspaper publisher, a major-league sports franchise owner, and a U.S. senator.

Madoff reportedly confessed to the Ponzi scheme once it became too difficult to continue attracting new investors, while early investors pinched by the recession in 2008 began withdrawing funds. In March 2009, he pleaded guilty to an 11-count criminal complaint, admitting to defrauding his more than 4,000 investors. As of this writing, he faced spending the rest of his life in prison.

How did Bernie Madoff manage to fool so many people for so long?

Well, it seems that for a con artist of his ilk, it's not only "the more the merrier," but "the more the easier." The Madoffs of the world craft an image of trustworthiness based on the business he's managed to bring in. This lures more victims, and so on. Since some reputable, intelligent, accomplished people had become Madoff's clients, more investors gullibly followed without taking a cold hard look at Madoff's financial track record and method of investing.

A first-person account of the seduction comes from a psychology professor who was one of Madoff's clients—and got burned in the flameout. Writing in the *Wall Street Journal* (Jan. 3, 2009), Stephen Greenspan (no relation to former Federal Reserve Board chairman Alan Greenspan) confessed that he'd neglected to do his own research into Madoff's investment services, and instead trusted in the judgments of the many smart people who'd preceded him.

Some insight on this behavioral phenomenon can be gleaned from *The Wisdom of Crowds* (Anchor Books, 2005), a stimulating book by James Surowiecki, business columnist with *The New Yorker* magazine. One of Surowiecki's examples of how people can make bad decisions is the "information cascade" about a hot new restaurant, whose quality people judge by the size of the crowd at the door, rather than the food, atmosphere, and service. Instead of relying on their own personally acquired knowledge, diners are influenced by the decisions other people have already made as a sign of quality. If the restaurant is popular, they reckon, it must be good.

By contrast, for people to make good decisions (on their own or as part of a group), they need to ask themselves four questions, listed on the facing page.

AM I DRAWING ON MY OWN FIRSTHAND KNOWL-
EDGE?

AM I GETTING INFORMATION FROM DIVERSE SOURCES?

AM I ACTING (OR DECIDING WHAT TO DO) BASED IN PART
ON WHATEVER FIRSTHAND EXPERIENCES I HAVE HAD?

AM I OVERLY INFLUENCED BY WHAT OTHER PEOPLE HAVE ALREADY
DONE IN SIMILAR CIRCUMSTANCES?

The answers to the first three questions should be yes, and to the last, no!

So when it comes to buying something or making a particular investment, consider the transaction on the basis of its own merits—not by the line at the door.

Establishing Contact

LET'S recall what we said earlier in this chapter: The key factor in victimization is simply whether one is exposed to an attempt.

As you make your way up the economic ladder, you will receive more and more pitches from people with something to sell—simply because your increasing spending ability makes you a more attractive consumer. You'll receive ever more advertisements and direct solicitations by mail or email, telephone or via some of the groups to which you belong. Some of these offers are bound to be bogus. That's why healthy skepticism is always warranted when someone approaches you with a plan that seems too good to be true.

One method to lower your profile as a potential target is to limit your exposure to swindle attempts. Check out the list on the next page.

Lower Your Profile

1 **Telephone.** Legitimate telemarketing is big business. Fraudulent telemarketing is big business, too. The Federal Bureau of Investigation estimates there are 14,000 illegal telephone sales operations in our nation bilking consumers out of as much as $40 billion each year.

The best way to avoid getting telemarketing calls that you don't want is to contact the Federal Trade Commission and have your phone number placed on the National Do Not Call Registry. You can register online at www.donotcall.gov or call toll-free, 1-888-382-1222 (TTY 1-866-290-4236). If you register by phone, you must call from the number you want to register. If you register online, you must provide an email address for confirmation.

2 **Mail.** Although swindlers may work from bona fide mailing lists, more often they purchase "mooch" or "sucker" lists from other crooks containing the names of known victims. Names on these lists can cost as much as $10 to $100 each, depending on how gullible a victim has been in the past. Telemarketers use the same or similar calling lists.

Mailings are generally used to prompt prospective victims to write or call for more information. A salesperson then contacts the people who inquire about the promotion, to close the deal. This technique is more effective than a "cold call" because the mark has demonstrated an interest by responding. In some cases, a salesperson may call to notify a person that he or she almost passed by a great opportunity by not responding to the mailing.

3 **Affinity Groups.** As the Madoff scandal demonstrates, another way swindlers try to attract prospective victims is by using the leverage afforded by being affiliated with an affinity group. This is an organization or association with shared interests, backgrounds, or beliefs. Examples include family, religious, ethnic, community, and professional groups. People are generally more trusting of others if a common bond exists between them. If a swindler is not directly connected to an affinity group, he or she may approach one or more prominent members in the group to gain their trust. The swindler then uses the trust placed in the prominent members by the group to gain the trust of others in the group. Utilizing referrals eliminates the need for the swindler to find new victims; the victims will find the swindler.

4 Internet. The Internet is an ideal tool for fraudsters. Simply by building an impressive and credible-looking website, posting a message on a bulletin board, joining a chat room discussion, or sending spam, an unscrupulous operator can reach a wide audience without spending a lot of time, effort, or money. And because of the relative anonymity of the Internet, crooks can remain essentially nameless and faceless—appearing and disappearing at will. Moreover, the Internet's rapid expansion provides a huge base of unsophisticated new users to exploit.

People often let down their guard when they are online. A person who may be properly wary of receiving unsolicited mailings or cold calls from unfamiliar salespersons may be less skeptical of a website he or she comes across while surfing the web. Unfortunately, many people readily accept at face value what they see and read on the web. Most of the fraud and abuse problems floating around in cyberspace are the same scams perpetrated over the phone or through the mail.

Then again, some instances of Internet duplicity build on on-line affinity groups. In recent years a dismaying variety of crimes and swindles have come to light involving Facebook and MySpace, not to mention the classified ads in craigslist.com. Whatever their value, such social networking sites also open the door to a merging of Internet anonymity and pseudo affinity, a ready-made formula for fraud.

Common Sales Tactics—Getting You to Say Yes!

AFTER making contact, the swindler turns to the primary objective: closing the deal. One crook explained his closing technique this way: "One hand goes up to the wall and starts painting pictures, while the other hand reaches for their checkbook."

Painting a rosy picture. Swindlers appear to be superb salespersons. They really aren't. But they are chronic liars. For example, a scam artist can tout a highly lucrative yet speculative investment as low risk—"guaranteed!" The honest salesperson must make sure an aggressive investment is appropriate and point out any inherent risks involved. But cheats purposely avoid such considerations.

Sense of Urgency. Typically a cheat will insist that you invest in whatever he or she is offering *right now*. The cheat may inform you that the investment is being offered for a limited time only or being offered to a limited number of people. Or, the cheat may claim that he or she is giving you a chance to get in on the "ground floor" before every Tom-Dick-and-Harry jumps on the bandwagon.

There are important reasons why the swindler wants you to act today. The simplest, of course, is that the swindler doesn't want to expend any more time or energy than needed to get your money. But there are other, just as compelling, reasons. The cheat doesn't want to give you a chance to talk to others, or investigate him or her, or research the investment. If you mention that you would like to consult with your attorney or accountant about the matter, the cheat may quip, "There isn't time for that," or "Can't you make your own investment decisions?" or "What would your accountant or lawyer know about this business? This is my livelihood, if you have questions, *ask me*!" If you mention that you need to discuss the proposition with your spouse, a cheat will have an equally quick retort. To a man: "Who wears the pants in your family?" and to a woman: "Do you let your husband run your life?"

The Bottom Line on Financial Fraud

THERE is an old adage in the business world: "Trust but verify." Given the high incidence of Ponzi schemes and other predatory practices out there, perhaps the best approach is one step beyond that: "Do not take anything for granted." Putting it another way: "Don't trust, and do verify."

> "You can be as romantic as you want about love, Hector; but you mustn't be romantic about money."
>
> —George B. Shaw

8

Couples and Money: Outsmarting Conflict

WHEN it comes to living under one roof with your loved one, money issues constitute the No. 1 reason why couples split. The sudden realities of the economic struggle as a married couple, involving spending decisions and budget constraints, can provide a rude awakening, especially for younger partners. Nearly 37 percent of women and 39 percent of men between ages 20 and 24 who marry will end up divorced, according to data from the National Center for Health Statistics. The numbers decline after that, but at any age, money management for couples is tricky territory. And as with a business partnership, the financial wellbeing of a marriage depends on the partners' communication and cooperation.

In the past few decades, two-income couples have become the norm. In addition, the earning power of women has increased as workplace inequities have been erased. For people in their twenties, women participate in the labor force at about the same rate as men. More recently, a majority of the workers who lost their jobs in the Subprime Recession of 2008 and 2009 were men.

Today the goal (if not always the reality) is typically for both spouses to share in the housekeeping, child-rearing and income-earning. Marriages function best when the partners are financially compatible—sharing the same philosophies, practices and goals about earning, spending and investing. But how will they know beforehand if they are compatible or not?

Pre-Nuptial Agreements (Formal and Informal)

ANY COUPLE contemplating marriage needs to have a pre-marital conversation about money matters. That is why churches or other sources of pre-marital counseling include this topic on their agenda. The goal is to bring possible points of conflict (and cooperation) out onto the table ahead of time, to minimize the potential for misunderstanding and conflict later, after the wedding.

Among the topics for any such conversation, one should be what happens if one party runs up credit-card debt after the marriage, and both parties are responsible for it. Sad to say, it is not unknown for someone exiting a marriage to max out the cards, leaving the debts behind.

Some couples preparing for marriage address the awkward and un-romantic topic of how to plan for who gets what in the event of a divorce. When a formal agreement seems called for, before the wedding date each party brings a lawyer to hash out the language, the contingency clauses, and the financial terms of the possible break-up of the marriage. (Yes, reality bites.)

When is a formal, legally drafted pre-nuptial legal agreement necessary? Whenever the two parties to the "nuptial" event—the wedding—have sharp contrasts in their financial positions. Such contrasts may arise from differing initial assets (including trust funds), incomes, an insurance settlement, or prospects of financial windfall (such as from an inheritance). These assets that pre-date the marriage will remain in the possession of the specific partner should the marriage fail.

By the same token, people without assets and with similar incomes and prospects do not need a legally drawn pre-nuptial agreement. But they still need to have an informal agreement, a mutually determined set of understandings about how money matters are to be worked out.

The House Account

WE TURN now to a practical financial arrangement that experience shows can improve the chances of making a marriage work. This is "the house account." The starting point for setting up this account is to view couple-wise money as yours, mine, and ours. "Yours" is your spouse's account. "Mine" is your own account. "Ours" is the house account—to cover shared income and expenses. The house account can be used for whatever it is that the two of you

are consuming together. That way, issues of control can fade into a fabric of sharing and cooperation.

Not that control issues will ever disappear entirely. But if a couple can get the house account running right, then the "yours" and "mine" accounts can cover the private or individual payments that are best left up to each person.

What kinds of payments or receipts are inherently more individual—for the "yours" and "mine" accounts? Some clear-cut items might be clothing, jewelry, or magazine subscriptions. These and many other examples are purchases whose benefits are not substantially shared by both parties. Also in this category would be a variety of more or less personal indulgences, such as cigarettes or lottery tickets. These are all solo enterprises.

The house account is for bills that cover goods and services used or enjoyed more or less equally. These might include electricity, heat, water, cable, phone, house repairs, lawn services, and other routine household expenses. For homeowners, this will probably also include property taxes and homeowners' insurance.

On the other hand, car insurance could well wind up as individual payments. It may not fall clearly into one or the other type of account. Suppose one party wants a flashy new car (with insurance rates to match), while the other is content with more modest wheels. Then the auto-buff might need to pay both the car payments and the higher portion of the insurance costs, instead of using the house account.

Examples of other kinds of payments that may also merit special treatment:

Kids' clothes. It sometimes happens that one parent places more stock on children's clothing than the other. Clearly some spending on this item is essential and should be covered by the house account.

An expensive self-powered lawnmower. Beyond just getting the lawn mowed, such vehicles offer the driver an opportunity to race around the yard singing cowboy songs, a private sort of pleasure.

Electricity usage. Some people want to buy dim bulbs and read by the fireplace, while others prefer well-lighted rooms (or well-heated ones, versus wearing sweaters all winter).

For these mixed cases, the house account can be used to pay for a base amount that benefits both partners. Then the person who wants more of the item (kids' clothes, a vehicle, bright lights) can "subsidize" the activity out of his or her individual account. How are such distinctions to be drawn? Through collaborative conversation and case-by-case negotiation.

In short, some kinds of ambiguous payments can be paid partly by the house account, and partly by a supplement or subsidy to be paid by one party out of his or her account.

Other issues requiring negotiation come readily to mind. Saving to buy a house, deciding how big a contribution to make to a 401(k) retirement account, or planning to fund a vacation—all these will need to be figured out to the mutual satisfaction of both parties. Not that such agreements are easy. But when plans about the future are not mutually arrived at, friction is sure to follow.

Financing the House Account—And the Other Two

LET'S LOOK now at specific cases. How much should each person contribute to the house account? Let's assume both parties agree on how much is needed for the house account, in light of specific expenses. In other words, a budget is set based on monthly income and monthly expenses.

Consider first a two-paycheck household. Suppose one party has an income of $50,000 a year and the other an income of $30,000. As the table below illustrates, absolute equality is not necessarily the goal. The goal is a working arrangement that feels fair to both parties. In this example, the two parties contribute the same percentage of their incomes—not the same amounts—to the house account. Many other variations might be suitable, as well, so long as both parties agree.

	Earnings	$ to House Acct.	$ to Own Acct.
Earnings by Person 1	$50,000		
$ to the House Account		$25,000	
Individual Account 1			$25,000
Earnings by Person 2	$30,000		
$ to the House Account		$15,000	
Individual Account 2			$15,000
Total	$80,000	$40,000	$40,000

What about the murkier issue of a homemaker, whether a house-husband or housewife, specifically when there are children to be raised? One approach, not unique to Japan but widely practiced there, is for a careerist "salary man" to bring his paycheck home and turn it over to his homemaker wife. She then makes the financial decisions and handles the payments and deposits.

In the absence of such a tradition, some middle ground will likely work just as well, provided that the house-person receives a stipend adequate to meet his or her individual expenditures. Here, as elsewhere in this chapter, the question of how large such a stipend should be can be amicably determined only through a friendly dialogue and trial and error.

Breakdowns and Tune-ups

S PEAKING of trial and error, what might lead a couple to conclude that the arrangements for the three accounts needed adjusting? Two quite different perspectives could be relevant here. One is efficiency, the other fairness.

In terms of efficiency, you will know something needs fixing when the money that goes into the house account isn't enough to cover the costs of the house bills. In that case, and resources permitting, both parties may need to pony up more money for the house account, perhaps in the same proportions as before.

Fairness, on the other hand, is harder to deal with, since it involves a range of issues in a relationship, including sharing, compassion, dependency, equality, and love. To further complicate the matter, one of the partners may consistently spend more out of his or her account on a regular basis, consistently coming up short before the end of the month.

In a real-world example, a lawyer and his obstetrician wife were tottering on the brink of divorce over his excessive spending. While earning substantially less than she, he tended to buy expensive luxuries that left the couple with tens of thousands of dollars in consumer debt. In couple therapy, the "house-account" approach was suggested and adopted, rescuing the marriage (at least as of this writing).

Nevertheless, the lawyer consistently runs out of money in his own account, because he remains a big spender, far out of proportion to what he contributes to the house account. The result is further conversation and negotiation, as the obstetrician tries to hold the line against such excesses.

The lesson is that the approach advocated in this chapter may be constructive and even invaluable—but it cannot solve all the money problems that afflict couples. Still, experience suggests that it is a good place to start.

A strong and lasting spousal relationship requires work and planning. So does preparing for that time when you will retire. That's the subject of the next chapter.

> "When I was young I thought that money was the most important thing in life; now that I am old I know that it is."
> —Oscar Wilde

9

Retirement Planning in One Lesson

ANOTHER new year is approaching, and you're figuring out what resolutions to make and seal in an envelope. You jot down a health goal: yoga at least three times a week. You scribble out a professional goal: either earning a raise and promotion by June or actively beginning a new job search. Then there's the unrealized goal that's been on your list for three years: traveling to Africa. You realize you've done nothing to save up the money, carve out the vacation time or tend to the research necessary to organize such a trip. But you vow that the coming year will be different, because you'll prepare far in advance and make the trip happen.

That's the key, of course, planning. You don't want to end up being 30 and never having seen much of the world outside of the borders of your own country. Thirty, all of a sudden, doesn't seem as far away as it once did. Although if someone were to ask you what you think you'll be doing at age 40, 50 or 60, you would draw a blank. Seventy? You gotta be kidding!

What if someone were to tell you that at 70 you'd probably still be slaving like a dog, dreaming of retirement? Well, for a great many Americans in this new century, that sort of possibility isn't as remote as it may have seemed 10 or 20 years ago, when the norm for retirement was age 65.

The traditional three pillars of retirement financing—pensions, Social Security, and personal saving—have come to look increasingly shaky as the basis for most Americans' retirement strategy. Here's why:

Retirement Mega-Trends

1 The number of workers covered by traditional gold-watch pensions (called "defined-benefit" pensions), paid by an employer after the worker retires, is decreasing. Instead, the old-fashioned pension is rapidly being eclipsed by 401(k) self-financing plans.

2 Future retirees cannot count on Social Security to cover as much of their expenses as it does for today's retirees. Why? Social Security is what might politely be termed "underfunded." In plain English, benefits for today's younger workers (this includes you) are virtually certain to be cut back over the next few decades.

3 As a matter of rising longevity, the retirement years represent a larger portion of life than ever before. A child born in the United States in 2005 could expect to live to 77.9 years—a new high for life expectancy in our nation, and an increase of 8.3 years over a half-century before, according to The Centers for Disease Control's National Center for Health Statistics. As death rates for certain leading causes of death continue to decline due to improving health education and treatment, life expectancy in America likely will continue to increase. That means you'll likely be living longer than members of the generations before you.

That's the good news. The bad news? Future retirees without sufficient savings may have to work longer. (If you doubt this, look around at many of today's seniors who thought they were about to retire, but then had to change their plans after the stock market tumbled, cracking their retirement nest eggs.)

4 Medical costs are rising faster than prices generally, which means that you must budget today for higher expenses in the future. At the same time, many companies are cutting back on retiree health benefits for their employees, leaving coverage gaps that early retirees must address on their own.

Save It!

THE UPSHOT is that your own individual savings plan is the key to whether you will have enough money to see you through your later years. To be realistic, young people often have to focus on immediate needs such as paying debts incurred for schooling, or establishing a separate household and accumulating some savings for marriage and raising a family.

But whatever can be put aside early will have that much longer to pile up tax-free and grow. Your goal should be the continued, uninterrupted funding of a savings plan in an amount you can reasonably afford. Whether for a house, college expenses, or (especially) retirement, there is a simple rule: *Save as much as you can as soon as you are financially able to do so*, because the magic of compound interest is much more powerful over longer periods of time.

This point is illustrated in the table below, which shows how large a sum even modest monthly savings can generate, if you begin early. For example, if you start saving $66 a month at age 25, the $31,680 you save by the time you are 65 will generate a nest egg of $100,000 (assuming an average annual return of five percent). But if you wait until 40, it will take $168 a month and a total set-aside of $50,400 to generate $100,000 as a nest egg at 65.

The 401(k) . . . And Its Cousins

AS TRADITIONAL pensions become ever scarcer among younger workers, the other type of employer-based retirement program, the 401(k), becomes

---

Table 1
How Much You Need to Invest to Reach $100,000 at Retirement
(Savings in a tax-deferred account earning a 5 percent rate of return)

Contributions Made from Age...	Monthly Contribution	Total Contribution
25 to 65	$66	$31,680
30 to 65	$88	$36,960
35 to 65	$120	$43,200
40 to 65	$168	$50,400
45 to 65	$243	$58,320
50 to 65	$374	$67,320
55 to 65	$644	$77,280

that much more important. Currently, some 50 million private-sector employees participate in 401(k)-type accounts, more than twice the number who use traditional pension plans.

The 401(k)-type accounts are known as "defined-contribution" plans. What is defined is not a monthly pension benefit for after you retire, but the amount you (and perhaps your employer) contribute into an investment account each month.

In addition to 401(k)s, the various other types of defined-contribution plans include 403(b)s for nonprofit organizations, 457 plans for state and local government employees, and Roth 401(k) plans (paid for with after-tax dollars, but which can be withdrawn after a certain age without being taxed). These variations on the basic model still share the same basic advantages.

The retirement benefit in a 401(k)-type plan is not directly tied to the employee's salary or years of service. Instead, it depends on the market value of the account at the time of retirement. *The employer assumes no liability for guaranteeing a specific benefit* and no obligation beyond making any promised contributions (such as matching funds) during an employee's years of service.

Still, some 70 percent of employees with 401(k) accounts received matching contributions from employers. The match formulas range as a rule from 25 to 100 percent of what the employee puts in, with 50 percent as the most common ratio. For example, an employee contributing 6 percent of her paycheck in such a plan could have it matched by 3 percent from the employer, for a total of 9 percent of her salary.

Tax Advantages

TO REPEAT, the salary-reduction option of a 401(k)-type plan allows an employee *to choose to have part of his or her salary go to a retirement fund rather than have it paid as salary today*. The tax advantages of this are twofold. First, earnings that you contribute are not counted in your taxable income. (The exception: Roth contributions are from after-tax income, but the withdrawals upon retirement will be tax-free.) Second, the investment returns earned in your account are also tax-deferred.

Employers may match your contribution in full or in part. As a result, you can earn a much higher return on your 401(k)-type investment than you could in comparable investments outside of the plan.

Three different one-word retirement plans for the generations who won't be able to draw benefits from the underfunded Social Security Trust Fund in their golden years:

A. LOTTERY
(As in, winning a jackpot.)

B. INHERITANCE
(As in, hoping their parents don't spend all their wealth on themselves before they die.)

C. DIY
(As in, putting a portion of every paycheck into a retirement account.)

Even if Your Employer Contributes Nothing . . .

MATCHING contributions from your employer make such plans an all but unbeatable investment. In essence, if your employer offers to contribute to your plan, deciding not to participate is akin to failing to accept a raise or a bonus.

But even if your employer does not match your contribution, the favorable tax treatment of your own investment, and of the earnings on it, still make it more attractive than most other methods of saving.

A Word About Independent Retirement Accounts

IF YOU want to supplement your 401(k), or you don't have access to one, you may want to open an Individual Retirement Account. There are now several types of plans available, including traditional IRAs, Roth IRAs, SIMPLE and SEP plans, Keoghs, and the newest addition, the solo 401(k). Each offers its own distinctive tax benefits. We'll focus here on the traditional IRA, because it is most commonly used.

As with 401(k)s, IRAs offer two important tax advantages. The investment income on an IRA contribution accumulates tax-free until the funds are withdrawn. Second, depending on your income and whether you participate in a company pension plan, your IRA contribution may be tax-deductible on federal and many state income-tax returns.

The maximum allowable contribution in 2009 is $5,000, or 100 percent of earned income, whichever is lower. If you file a joint tax return, you and your spouse may each contribute up to the maximum amount as long as your combined earnings cover the contributions.

Do You Need Help?

THE MESSAGE of this chapter is that you need to get started saving early and to make saving a priority. No one is saying those tasks are easy. But the new realities all tend to point in the same direction. If you want to have adequate resources in your retirement years, save now—and keep on saving until it hurts.

Over the long haul, the specific choices you make about savings and investment may be less important than simply getting started and putting some money away early on. (It's a vital habit to develop.) As we have seen in this chapter, tax treatment of your savings and investments is a key variable. Beyond that, the fine points are less important, with one big exception:

Whether on your own or through a financial adviser, you will want to avoid exorbitant "management fees" on your various accounts. These fees can range from .5 percent or less to more than 2 percent on your assets per year. If a financial adviser is taking additional fees besides, there will be still less in your account at the end of each year to grow at compound interest rates. Over time, the contrast in fees can make a surprising difference in how fast your investments grow—and how big a nest egg you will have later.

Should you hire a financial adviser? The limited space in this book does not permit a simple across-the-board answer. But one thing is sure: If you do it, do it with care and research, because financial advisers have a way of being even more interested in their own incomes than in your investments.

What would a good financial planner be likely to suggest? Diversify your investments between stocks (such as an "index fund" of the S&P 500) and bonds (also known as "fixed-income" securities). And hold a percentage equal to your *age* in bonds or money market accounts, the rest in stocks—e.g., if you're 30, hold 70 percent of your investments in a stock index fund.

10

Where Do You Want to Live?

"There's no place like home."
—Dorothy Gale

BUYING your first home has traditionally served as a milestone on your drive for financial independence. Nevertheless, events in recent years suggest that some of the benefits of home-ownership—not least among them freedom from raucous roommates—can be gained more cheaply in other ways.

In the midst of the Subprime Recession, which is in full sway as we write, it would be rash to tell you what you should do about buying a house. The long-time prescription on when to buy a house ("as soon as you can") no longer applies. By the same token, for the foreseeable future, the American Dream no longer automatically equates to owning your own home.

Yes, housing prices have plunged across the nation, and in that sense getting into a first house is more affordable than it was at the peak of the housing bubble in 2005. Still, the 20 percent required for a down payment on a house costing a few hundred thousand dollars is still a lot of money.

If anything, the direction of the housing market has switched. Recent college graduates, who may have been tempted to seek home loans in 2005 or 2006, move back in increasing numbers to live with their parents, to weather the financial fallout.

Whatever the state of the economy, certain basic questions about housing remain the same. To sort out your options here, we now consider three decisions every adult faces after leaving the parental nest or finishing schooling: What kind of insurance will you need? Where do you want to live? Should you rent or should you buy?

Homeowner's (and Renter's) Insurance

WHETHER you rent or whether you buy, you will need some form of insurance to protect against accidents, mishaps or theft. Insurance against the risk of the loss of one's residence from fire is one of the oldest types of insurance. Modern methods of heating and cooking and modern construction methods have greatly reduced the risk of residential fires. However, other risks have increased as a result of rising rates of crime, and litigation over accidents.

Most owner-occupants purchase "homeowner's insurance" that covers these risks. It also covers losses of personal property (including property carried by the insured when not at home, such as a camera stolen during a vacation), legal judgments in favor of visitors who are injured on the owner-occupant's property, living expenses incurred if the residence becomes uninhabitable, and water damage. Umbrella personal-liability coverage may be offered under the homeowner's policy.

If you are a renter, you should purchase "tenant's insurance," which provides the same coverage as homeowner's insurance except for that on the structure itself. Here, as well, you will want to list (or better yet, videotape) your possessions, to support any claims in case of, say, a robbery. You should inspect the policy and eliminate any conditions that would void the insurance in the event of a claim. Know when policies expire. Do not depend entirely on your agent to advise you of the policy's expiration date.

Depending on the value of your house, homeowner's insurance may cost between $500 and $2,000 a year, or more. Note that this coverage needs to be enough to rebuild the house in case of fire, flood or other natural disaster, or a gas explosion—*not* the market value of the house. What you are trying to provide (and are required to provide, until your mortgage is paid off), is a payment that would cover the rebuilding of your house on your lot. A renter's policy would cost commensurately less, of course, since what is being insured is your possessions, not your real property.

Where Do Americans Want to Live?

As **THE** Detroit-case makes clear, there is more to buying a house than price alone. Even with current prices below $10,000 for some properties, you may not want to buy a house there. The local economy is in agony, the weather is harsh, and the downtown lights are dim.

This, at any rate, is how the Detroit area is perceived, judging by a recent Pew Research survey of 2.260 adults. It ranked the Detroit area last out of 30 large metropolitan areas as a place to live. As the table shows, the top five areas were Denver, San Diego, Seattle, Orlando, and Tampa. Whereas 43 percent of those surveyed said they would live in Denver, only 8 percent said that about Detroit.

America's Most Popular Metro Areas

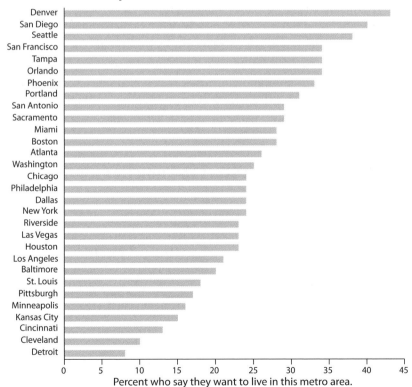

Percent who say they want to live in this metro area.

Source: Pew Research Center, "For Nearly Half of America, Grass Is Greener Somewhere Else," January 29, 2009.

Of course, such preferences do not necessarily translate into migration flows. Job availabilities and family ties can be decisive factors as to where younger workers end up settling down. Also, younger Americans are more comfortable living in large cities than their elders. But when their family circumstances change—above all, when children arrive and reach school age—most families would prefer to move to suburbia or a small town.

What such survey results suggest is a tendency for younger Americans to relocate to medium-sized metro areas in the West and South, where nature feels accessible, the pace is a little slower, and some semblance of community spirit can thrive.

Whether house prices in such high-amenity destinations will prove reasonable remains to be seen. But one thing seems certain: As the example of Detroit makes clear, house prices, even after the recession, are only one ingredient in your choice of locations.

For that matter, Detroit's economic troubles also point up a surprising finding of some studies of income differences between homeowners and renters. We touched upon migration as a stairway to opportunity a moment ago. As it happens, researchers at MIT have found a tendency for *renters* to have greater income-growth over the duration of their careers, seemingly because when economic opportunity beckoned, they were free to move, without being tied down by a house whose price had plummeted. To stay flexible, this seems to suggest, rent don't buy.

When Do House Prices Start to Look Reasonable?

ARE THERE reliable rules of thumb to consider as to when it makes more sense to buy than to rent? A traditional approach (before the housing bubble turned buyers into investment speculators) was to compare monthly housing costs to rental costs. When you have totaled up all the costs (including utilities, taxes and mortgage payments) you may find that it costs about as much a month to rent as to buy. Then the decision gets down to personal preferences.

For example, some people want nothing to do with the endless upkeep and responsibilities that come with buying a house. For them, apartment living is the preferred option. For others, the pleasures of ownership, doing-it-yourself, and watching equity grow lead to an opposite course. In other words, given a certain rough parity of monthly costs, the buy-or-rent decision gets down to other factors.

Certainly the affordability of houses in many areas has improved sharply, given the plummeting market prices. Judging by the Case-Shiller Index of 20 large urban housing markets, the nationwide fall in median house prices from 2006 to January 2009 was a stunning 27 percent. In some areas where prices had risen most (Florida; Las Vegas, Nevada; Southern California), the decline was even larger.

As we write these words in 2009, house prices have tumbled in relation to personal income and to rental costs. As foreclosed properties are auctioned off, and buyers in conventional markets can afford to be choosy (since it is a buyer's market), house prices should continue falling, making them ever more affordable. Beyond the painful horizon of the Subprime Recession, then, lies a panorama of more economical housing. When the time is right for you, the traditional reasons for wanting to buy a house will kick in. At that point it may still make sense for you to avoid the burdens and responsibilities of home ownership. But inflated house prices—typified by the mid-decade housing bubble—probably won't be the reason.

The bottom line: The best reason to buy a house is probably that it provides *shelter*. When a house is viewed as an investment, recent values of the Case-Shiller index make clear that at current prices, housing rivals the stock market for disappointing performance. Since 1994, when prices were moderate, the nationwide increase in median house prices has grown at an annualized rate of 4.7 percent. Since the average inflation rate was 2.5 percent, the inflation-adjust rise in house prices was 2.2 percent a year. (Brett Arends, "Is Your Home a Good Investment?" *The Wall Street Journal*, May 27, 2009).

Against that rate of appreciation, you have to allow for a number of costs, including property taxes (about 1 percent a year, on average), the mortgage rate (if any), upkeep, and the opportunity cost of your down-payment and any monthly mortgage payments. What's left, roughly speaking, is a roof over your head: the imputed rental value of your house as shelter.

When the time comes for you to think about the choice, you might wish to obtain AIER's in-depth analysis, *Homeowner or Tenant? How to Make a Wise Choice*. It provides worksheets and a detailed look at mortgages and financing. (The cost is $8; call (888) 528-1216, or visit www.aier.org/bookstore.)

"The world is more

malleable than you think

and it's waiting for you

to hammer it

into shape."

—Bono

Next Steps...

KEEP TAKING CLASSES, INCLUDING FULL GRADUATE PROGRAMS IF THEY SUIT YOU, BUT ALSO ONE-WEEKEND WORKSHOPS, TO BUILD YOUR SKILLS. CONTINUING YOUR EDUCATION NOT ONLY WILL IMPROVE YOUR COMPETITIVE POSITION IN THE WORKFORCE AND MARKETPLACE, IT WILL HELP YOU FULFILL YOUR DESTINY, WHATEVER THAT MAY BE.

NETWORK! THE MORE FRIENDSHIPS AND ASSOCIATIONS YOU MAINTAIN OUTSIDE YOUR OWN WORKPLACE, THE BETTER YOU WILL MANAGE TO LAND ON YOUR FEET SHOULD YOUR CURRENT JOB COME TO AN END. BEYOND THAT, KEEPING YOUR EAR TO THE GROUND WILL HELP YOU FIGURE OUT WHETHER YOU MIGHT BE BETTER OFF DOING SOMETHING ELSE, INSIDE OR OUTSIDE YOUR PRESENT OCCUPATION OR INDUSTRY.

BE POSITIVE, DESPITE EVERYTHING.

Index

About AIER

American Institute for Economic Research (AIER) conducts independent, scientific, economic research to educate individuals, thereby advancing their personal interests and those of the nation.

The Institute, founded in 1933, represents no fund, concentration of wealth, or other special interests. Advertising is not accepted in its publications. Financial support for the Institute is provided primarily by the small annual fees from several thousand sustaining members, by receipts from sales of its publications, by tax-deductible contributions, and by the earnings of its wholly owned investment advisory organization, American Investment Services, Inc. Experience suggests that information and advice on economic subjects are most useful when they come from a source that is independent of special interests, either commercial or political.

The provisions of the charter and bylaws ensure that neither the Institute itself nor members of its staff may derive profit from organizations or businesses that happen to benefit from the results of Institute research. Institute financial accounts are available for public inspection during normal working hours of the Institute.

The Benefits of
AIER MEMBERSHIP

If you enjoyed this book, you'll love AIER's newsletter publications. With a staff of expert researchers, AIER is able to offer valuable insight on a wide array of economic and personal finance issues.

Research Reports provide concise discussion concerning a wide range of current issues. One article each month is devoted to analyzing changes in economic activity.

Economic Bulletins present in-depth treatment and analysis of topics pertaining to economics, fiscal policy, retirement, and personal finance.

For more information about AIER membership, **please call us toll free at (888) 528-1216.**

Mention this publication to receive a discount on your annual membership fee. Sign-up online by visiting our website, www.aier.org

publications currently available

Personal Finance

The A-Z Vocabulary for Investors
Coin Buyer's Guide
Homeowner or Tenant? How to Make a Wise Choice
How to Avoid Financial Fraud
How to Avoid Financial Tangles
How to Give Wisely: A Donor's Guide to Charitable Giving
How to Invest Wisely
How to Make Tax-Saving Gifts
How to Read a Financial Statement
How to Use Credit Wisely
If Something Should Happen:
   How to Organize Your Financial and Legal Affairs
Life Insurance: From the Buyer's Point of View
Sensible Budgeting with the Rubber Budget Account Book
Start Here: Getting Your FInancial Life on Track
What You Need to Know About Mutual Funds
What Your Car Really Costs:
   How to Keep a Financially Safe Driving Record

Retirement And Estate Planning

The Estate Plan Book—with 2001 Supplement
How to Build Wealth with Tax-Sheltered Investments
How to Choose Retirement Housing
How to Cover the Gaps in Medicare:
   Health Insurance and Long-Term Care Options for the Retired
How to Plan for Your Retirement Years
How to Produce Savings in the Administration of an Estate
What You Need to Know about Social Security

Money And Banking

The Collapse of Deposit Insurance
Gold and Liberty
Money: Its Origins, Development, Debasement, and Prospects
The Pocket Money Book:
   A Monetary Chronology of the United States
Prospects for a Resumption of the Gold Standard

General Economics

The AIER Chart Book
The Constitutional Protection of Property Rights: America and Europe
Forecasting Business Trends
The Future of the Dollar
The Global Warming Debate: Science, Economics, and Policy
On the Gap between the Rich and the Poor
Property Rights: The Essential Ingredient for Liberty and Progress
Prospects for Reforming the IMF and the World Bank
Reconstruction of Economics
The United States Constitution:
   From Limited Government to Leviathan